The ICO Approach

A Beginner's Guide to Understanding Cryptocurrency ICO

Martin Quest

© **Copyright 2018 - All rights reserved.**

The content contained within this book may not be reproduced, duplicated or transmitted without direct written permission from the author or the publisher.

Under no circumstances will any blame or legal responsibility be held against the publisher, or author, for any damages, reparation, or monetary loss due to the information contained within this book. Either directly or indirectly.

Legal Notice:

This book is copyright protected. This book is only for personal use. You cannot amend, distribute, sell, use, quote or paraphrase any part, or the content within this book, without the consent of the author or publisher.

Disclaimer Notice:

Please note the information contained within this document is for educational and entertainment purposes only. All effort has been executed to present accurate, up to date, and reliable, complete information. No warranties of any kind are declared or implied. Readers acknowledge that the author is not engaging in the rendering of legal, financial, medical or professional advice. The content within this book has been derived from various sources. Please consult a licensed professional before attempting any techniques outlined in this book.

By reading this document, the reader agrees that under no circumstances are is the author responsible for any losses, direct or indirect, which are incurred as a result of the use of information contained within this document, including, but not limited to, — errors, omissions, or inaccuracies.

About the Author

Martin Quest is an investor in the world of Bitcoin and cryptocurrency. Having made every rookie mistake in the book, he wants to help you navigate some of the initial pitfalls of this brand-new world. If holding can help him become a better investor, then perhaps it can do the same for you.

Table Of Contents

Chapter one: Introduction
Definition Of Initial Coin Offering
History of ICOs
Chapter 2: ICOs in Detail
How ICOs Work
What is an ICO presale period?
Pros of an ICO presale
Cons of an ICO presale
Maximizing Your Profits If The ICO Takes Off
Secure the bonus tokens
Hold and sell some technique
Keep things simple

Chapter Three: How to Pick a Winning ICO
Issues to Consider
1. Consider the team behind the ICO project
2. Carefully evaluate the white paper
3. What is the token needed for?
4. Social media and online presence
5. Is the ICO a hard cap or unlimited?
6. Check the quality of the codes

Chapter Four: How to get started
Know your customer protocol
Importance of KYC compliance for an ICO
How one can ensure KYC compliance
KYC steps

Crypto wallets
The Working Mechanism Of Cryptocurrency Wallets
Where Can You Get A Cryptocurrency Wallet?
Single Currency Or Multicurrency Use?
Are the crypto wallets secured?
Which are the best wallets?

Legal Status Of Icos In Various Countries

Perceived Challenges With ICOs

Progressive Countries In Terms Of ICOs

The future of ICOs in various countries

Registration with ICO
   What is gas in ICO?

MetaMask Wallet

Benefits of MetaMask

Chapter Five: Things to Avoid

Exit Scams

Identifying Exit Scams

Multi-Level Marketing Systems

Characteristics of Multi-Level Marketing Systems.

Regulation

Chapter Five: Wrapping It Up

Step in ICO Trading

Tips on Trading ICO Coins

Conclusion

References

Chapter one: Introduction

Definition Of Initial Coin Offering

Initial coin offering, commonly known as ICO, is the mechanism used to raise funds for financingcryptocurrency-related ventures and it is mostly used by startups as a way of evading the regulated capital-raising mechanisms used by banks or venture capitalists. For example, the Ethereum cryptocurrency project has already raised a lot of money in ICO. This investment model is closely related to Initial Public Offering (IPO) whereby interested investors purchase shares of a certain company. In ICO, the resulting coins are called tokens and they can be equated with the shares of a company that are sold to the investors. ICO has dominated the blockchain community, and many view ICO projects as securities that are unregulated. This can enable the founders to raise the capital required to undertake a certain crypto venture. To make it simple, crowdsourcing eliminates the hustle that is very common in the capital venture process. In every ICO campaign, a given cryptocurrency percentage is sold to the initial funders of the project as an exchange for a legal tender or another cryptocurrency like Bitcoin.

Every cryptocurrency startup must create an elaborate plan in its white paper explaining what the project is about, the problems that the project will solve after its completion, the amount of money needed to fund the venture, and the percentage of the coin that the pioneers will keep for themselves if the project succeeds. However, if the venture fails, the funds are returned to the financers and the ICO is said to have been unsuccessful. If the funds are enough, the project is initiated or the funds can be used to complete the project.

Generally, ICOs can be easily structured with the aid of technologies like ERC20 Token Standards, which ease the process of developing any cryptographic assets. Investors contributeto the ICO development by sending their funds in the form of Ether or Bitcoin to a set smart contract that can store their funds and, later, distribute the equivalent value of the new token.

Anyone can participate in an ICO because this venture has few restrictions, if any, assuming the fact that the token is not a security. Compared to the global pool that many investors find themselves in, with ICOs one can easily raise astronomical profits if things go well. However, there is a large margin of risk because they are extremely speculative since most of them raise pre-product money. But before discussing ICOs in detail, let us look at the historical context of how the entire trend started.

History of ICOs

The year 2014 turned to be one of the most dramatic points in crypto history because this was the time the ICO projects begun. Earlier on, many projects employed the crowd-sale model to fund their projects. A good example is Ripple, which pre-mined about one billion XRP tokens which were sold to potential investors in exchange for Bitcoin or fiat currencies. Early in 2014, Ethereum raised about 18 million dollars and this turned out to be the largest ICO completed at that time. The DAO was the initial attempt at raising funds for an upcoming token on the Ethereum system and it aimed at creating a decentralized and elaborate organization that would also fund other blockchain projects. However, the decisions and governance of the coin would be executed by the pioneers themselves.

DAO became a great success and managed to raise more than $150 million. However, due to much technical vulnerability, an unknown hacker broke into the system and drained millions from the DAO organization. The foundation opted to still focus forward despite this drawback. After the failure of the attempt to raise money to fund tokens using the Ethereum platform, the blockchain community realized that it was easier to raise the tokens compared to following the venture capital funding model. The ERC20 standards make the process of developing ICO tokens easy in the Ethereum platform which is blockchain based. When Ethereum opened the door for smart contracts, it unveiled a great potential for a generation of ICOs. With the ease of use of this system on top of a few regulations that have been set, startups have raised a large amount of funds within a short period and Aragon, as a perfect example, managed to raise about $25 million within 15 minutes. Out of the simplicity of creating tokens on the Ethereum blockchain platform, a wide variety of tokens have been created to serve different purposes.

Chapter 2: ICOs in Detail

We always encounter many news about ICO ventures, but due to insufficient explanations in these news publications, it becomes difficult for many people to understand everything about ICO in detail. This eBook sets out to explain how ICOs work and why they are opted for as a fundraising model.

How ICOs Work

An initial coin offering can be viewed as a refined form of crowdfunding that has emerged outside the common financial system. This technique has enabled companies to undertake some great projects and, through crowdfunding, they have secured the funding required to fund their projects.

ICO can be said to be the cryptocurrency version of crowdfunding that has been well incorporated into the crypto world, and this model is here to stay. An ICO event extends up to one or more weeks whereby everyone is always allowed to buy new tokens in exchange for Bitcoin or any other established cryptocurrency. Every ICO has a specific limit or goal for the project funding and this means that every single token always has a pre-determined price that does not change throughout the initial coin offering periods; this is what makes the supply of the token static.

There can also be a static supply with a dynamic funding objective, whereby the distribution of the token will depend on the amount of funds received and this results ina higher token price if the project receives more funding.

What is an ICO presale period?

As implied by the name, pre-ICO sales give the investors a chance to buy the tokens before the onset of the official sales. A pre-ICO sale is based on a smart contract to keep the funds separate from the official sale to avoid confusion. Generally, few funds are gathered at the presale stage because, during this period, the ICO tokens are sold at a lower price on top of certain bonuses to the investors. Different organizations initiate the presale for different reasons. Just to give you a glimpse, these are some of the common reasons why companies initiate presales prior to the official opening of the crowdfunding.

- It is used as a promotional tool by most of the companies. An ICO is always an easy way of distributing capital and ensuring that the investors will stand for the upcoming project. An ICO presale is more of "buy one, get one for free" kind of approach. The presale thus ends up raising awareness about the ICO. This is always the best period to invest in an ICO because the tokens are sold at a lower price because the companies give offers that will attract the attention of the investors. After the implementation of the project, the companies increase their profits after getting enough long-term investors.

- Some of the companies may opt to initiate a presale as a way of testing the potential that the ICO has. Simply, they aim to understand whether people are interested in their ICO and whether they are willing to invest in it.

- This undertaking is also a tool that attracts and keeps long-term investors' whole belief in the idea, products, or services offered by the company.

Generally, the main aim of a presale in an ICO is to attract angel investors who fund the operational costs of the company when the white papers and roadmaps are being worked out.

While an ICO presale is a great way that the company can raise some funds to jumpstart its operations, the company can also be hurt, especially if many tokens are sold at a low price during the offer period. Most of the companies begin their presale period about a month before the official release of the ICO, but such an opportunity cannot be available to every person because the presale may be accompanied by some limitations. To participate in this, one needs a KYC (know your customer) approval and secondly, to meet the minimum amount needed. For instance, the lowest set amount could be $10,000 and the maximum amount cap per person could be about $1,000,000.

Pros of an ICO presale

- Liquidity. As an investor, one can trade tokens in secondary markets instead of fixing up a given value in equity of a certain company.
- Ensures there is a good distribution of capital. When an ICO presale is well

organized, it opens a great door that facilitates allocation of capital in a rational manner. With ICOs, there is no any demographic or geographic barrier and anyone can be involved in this investment, regardless of their nationality.

- A crowd-funded ICO startup has many supporters. In ICOs, many people are involved and incentivized to be participants of the project and the company ends up getting many supporters who are committed and engaged with the happenings of the company.

Cons of an ICO presale

- Many scams and frauds. Scammers sometimes take advantage of such opportunities to illegally raise money which ends up in the pockets of certain people and not in the project that was initially presented to the vibrant investors.

- Restrictions and risks. Economists always argue that the greater the margin of risk, the greater the reward. In simple terms, very risky projects always have a high potential for producing great returns. Based on this risk, it is advisable for one to be cautious when investing in ICOs because some projects may end up failing and the presale investors' end up losing large sums of money, especially when the companies fail to refund the investors.

- Loyalty related issues. In the presale phase, most investors buy large amounts of tokens at a cheaper price because of the favorable offers that are used to attract investors at the beginning. When the prices rise, most investors immediately sell all their tokens, thus defaulting the company.

For any ICO to succeed and bring awesome profits, some key parameters need to be accounted for. These are some of the key things that one must pay attention to when deciding which a good is or a bad presale and whether it is worthwhile to invest in or not:

- Reviews. When considering whether to buy a certain product or undertake a certain investment, reviews act as a guide to whether the product is worth it or not. Presale ICOs are not an exception to this determinant. As an investor, make sure that you check all the critiques and opinions given by the investors who have preceded you in investing in the presale under question. Out of the reviews, make sure that you have a general idea or glimpse of what other people perceive and think about the ICO. This will act as your navigator and you will finally end up making a wise decision.

- Funding by well-established companies. Ensure that you carry out your research to find out if the company that is behind the pre-ICO in question has any parent organization or partnership with a bigger company. This is yet another criterion that indicates whether the ICO company is legit or not. More often, ICO presales that have partnered with well-established companies end up being very successful. Such ICOs have a lower probability of fraudism and are likely to have exceptional offers.

- Rumors. Always keep your ear open to what people are saying about a certain ICO presale in social media and other forums. Consider whether people find the ICO presale trustworthy, suspicious, or interesting. Even if rumors are not a credible source of information, sometimes they can bear some leaked information about a given ICO. At the same time, remember to read what ICO experts are saying about a certain presale.

- Hype. Make sure that you have a good understanding of what the product is and what the company is offering and try to figure out whether it is worth that. Concurrently, make sure that you avoid the "too good" kinds of offers as most such exciting projects end up being big scams that rob people their hard-earned money. If the ICO presale is good, you will encounter it in social media and various cryptocurrency forums. A good presale will also have a good customer support desk that is responsive and ready to answer all customer questions.

On the other hand, after the presale period, the ICO is then released to the public whereby anyone can buy the tokens if they are willing and able to meet the established requirements. During this going-public-period, the tokens are always sold at a higher price when compared to the presale period where only a few people were willing to risk their funds in investing at that initial point.

After carrying out your research, settle on a certain ICO that you are confident enough to invest in and if the ICO is good enough, think of making a presale purchase of the coins because, at this point, you will be able to buy the tokens at a relatively cheaper price, regardless of the quantum of tokens that you need. Sometimes, at this point, willing investors may be offered up to a 50 percent discount and if one purchases a handsome number of tokens at this point, one is assured of reaping great profits when the tokens are released publicly where their value becomes a multiple of the original value at the presale period.

The bottom line on this issue of ICO presale and public sales is that buying the tokens before the official launchoffers more value for your investment than buying them after launching.

Maximizing Your Profits If The ICO Takes Off

An ICO is a great venture with amazing profits if it is well undertaken. For example, if you purchased $100-worth of BTC on 2011, it would have cost $0.30 per BTC, and with your $100 investment, you would have received 333.33 BTC then. If you kept these Bitcoins for seven good years, by 2017 the price of BTC had shot up to about $11,000 and your initial $100 would be currently worth about $3.5m. By simple mathematics, this is a 35, 000 percent profit within seven years! This makes ICOs and the entire crypto world one of the most profitable investments in history. This meteoric rise of Bitcoin excites investors about cryptocurrencies and with heavy and smart investment by buying promising tokens. But just to guide you, this is how you can grow your crypto investments and maximize profits and make moneywhen the ICO of your choice takes off.

We have seen much about ICOs, and when you participate in an ICO, you receive coins or tokens as a contributor to the project. Now, after receiving the tokens, you must get your investment back and maximize profits. How do you retrieve your investment after receiving the tokens? How do you maximize profits after receiving the ICO coins? Among others, these are some of the common questions that every ICO investor cannot avoid asking themselves. These are good questions and, in this eBook, you will learn how to do all this as a newbie in ICO investing.

The tokens and the coins are also commonly referred to as altcoins and are usually issued by ICO- based projects. Thisvaries from one platform to another and different tokens are stored in their corresponding wallets. For example, Bitcoin has several variants with different wallets like Trezor, Armory,and Electrum where one can store the tokens. Foe Ethereum-based tokens, they are usually ERC20s tokens and MEW and MyEtherWallet are the best wallets to store them. Other token variants have their specific wallets depending on their platforms.

Understanding this issue of wallets for various tokens is very important so that you can store your tokens in the appropriate wallet, and this is always the first step in turning your altcoins into liquid cash. To protect your investment, it is important that you transfer the altcoinsfrom the company's or project's ICO page to your personal wallets, which are more secure. This is more like putting your stock bonds in a vault. After this, the next thing is always to wait until the altcoin you have invested in is listed in the exchange system. In simple terms, an exchange is a market where you can sell or buy commodities and this system is more like the stock exchange. Here, your altcoins work like the stocks.

Secure The Bonus Tokens

Many ICOs tend to offer bonuses as incentives to investors who contribute early, before the ICO is officially launched publicly. For instance, the minimum requirement of investing in the LiveEdu ICO in the initial stages was $3. But at this stage, one qualified for at least a 25 percent bonus if they invested 50 percent or more and that is why serious investors should invest in the pre-ICO stage because, with the bonuses, you are assured of receiving more tokens in addition to what you have targeted for your investment.

Hold And Sell Some Technique

After receiving the tokens, you can start trading them on exchange for different cryptocurrencies like ETH or BTC or, sometimes, cash. After receiving the coins, a good idea would be to immediately sell about 30 percent of the tokens so that you can recoup your initial investment and then hold the remaining 70 percent for some time before you think of selling them again. Still, the cryptocurrency market is very volatile and a lot of uncertainty and fear surrounds the ICO tokens. However, this should not hinder you from investing.

Keep things simple

Investing in ICOs comes with risk, but never allow these risks to force you into overthinking; In fact, risk-taking is common in every business. Always do your best and make sure you carry out some research before investing in a certain token. In this, you do not need to use some complicated scientific modelsto predict which tokens will yield great returns. You just need to understand a few things about the product offering before investing in it. And to make huge profits, keep your eye on promising tokens and make sure you are involved early enough.

Chapter Three: How to Pick a Winning ICO

The cryptocurrency sector is a rapidly growing market with a very high potential but before you jump into this market with astonishing profits, it is very crucial for you to understand how to choose a good ICO to invest in. The success of any ICO coin is influenced by several aspects and in this chapter we will look at how you can choose a winning ICO.

At this point, it is worthwhile to mention stories of failed ICOs like the Mycelium ICO, whose developers disappeared after raising the money. It was afterward reported that they used the funds for their vacation. The increased lack of regulation of this sector may be the reason $7 million was hacked and stolen from the Coin Dash's ICO. This happened just before the sale of the tokens began. The hacker broke into the system and the ICO wallet address was replaced with the hackers' address.

Based on the above incidents, ICOs are a very risky way of fundraising and it is important for you to take precautions by never attempting to invest what you cannot afford to lose in case the project fails, because you will have difficulty in getting your money back. Before investing in a certain ICO, consider the following issues.

Issues to Consider

1. Consider the team behind the ICO project

When researching on the coin to invest in, always check everythingrelated to the development team plus the body that offers advice to the developers. Scrutinize the individual members of the team by considering their knowledge and experience in starting and running ICO-based projects and their overall experience in the cryptocurrency world. You can visit their LinkedIn profiles, Google the names of the individuals involved, and look for any famous names on the advisory board. Generally, check the ICO projects they have been involved in; you can research further and check how successful their earlier projects have been.

2. Carefully evaluate the white paper

Most investors never bother to read the white paper, even if it contains all the necessary information about the upcoming ICO project. As an investor, always make sure that you read the entire white paper and make sure that you identify the negative and positive aspects of the project and include this in your research. After reading the whole white paper, make sure you can explain what the project is bringing to the world and make sure you have a good grasp of what ICO you are investing in.

3. What is the token needed for?

An ICO is essentially meant for the creation of a new token dedicated for a specific project. The most evident question here is what the token is meant for. Why aren't Ethereum and Bitcoin sufficient enough to serve as the tokens of the project being undertaken? You must ask yourself such questions because some projects just make up a scummy story to back up their venture. However, remember that an ICO cannot be a perfect ICO if it has no dedicated token. These questions still must be asked about the usage of blockchain technology on that project.

4. Social media and online presence

As an investor, when you Google the name of the company, you should be able to find sufficient information regarding it. Check out the press releases of the company, their blog, and their social media activities. With the information from those sources, you will be able to gauge their trustworthiness and monitor their activities. Also, remember to check the opinions of your fellow investors on the platforms that have been dedicated to the cryptocurrency investors regarding the ICO project in question.

5. Is the ICO a hard cap or unlimited?

In past years, a hard cap and open ICOs did not have as muchimpact as today. An open cap gives investors the opportunity to send an unlimited amount of funds to the ICO project wallet. On this issue, many tend to forget that if many coins are circulating, the token becomes less unique and afterward there may be difficulty in trading the coin because the demand will be low. On the other hand, make sure that you are not the only person investing in a certain project because exchanges always have little interest with the projects that raise little because this makes it difficult for you to trade the tokens after they are released.

6. Check the quality of the codes

If you have basic programming skills, you can apply the knowledge here. The quality of the ICO project developer can be understood by just carrying out a simple analysis of the codes. As a non-techie in the programming world, you can simply evaluate the quality of the code by checking the consistency of the code.

ICOs are becoming a main stream fundraising method and, based on the many upcoming projects that are using ICOs. However, by following these key guidelines, you can easily pick out all the negative and positive aspects and be able to make a wise decision on which ICO project to invest in.

Chapter Four: How to get started

Know Your Customer Protocol

Verification is a great challenge all over, and the digital world is not an exception. Companies take strict measures to scrutinize and verify the identity of their clients and at the same time, customers are becoming more cautious and sensitive with most companies, especially when it comes to giving out their information, which is sensitive, or when investing with a given company. In the cryptocurrency world, various regulators in various countries across the globe are becoming more interested with ICOs and this has brought a lot of uncertainty to both those who are offering the ICOs and those who are willing to invest in them.

There are many reasons why one should opt to invest in ICOs and this ranges from the speculation that the value of the coin will rise to the belief of high utilityfor a new piece of crypto. Unfortunately, lack of regulation in the crypto space means that anyone willing to invest in a given project always feel they are risking being treated like money launderers. Because, most of the time, legislation may be unclear or absent, know your customer (KYC) is a broadly used concept in the finance world globally.

Currently, the regulation of ICOs is based on KYC and this has turned out to be a necessity to ensure that potential investors can legally and willingly participate in the ICO investment. This is mainly because scamming activities have been spotted and the KYC-related policies and issues that have been implemented within the financial institutions have been incorporated into the ICO sector.

Importance Of KYC Compliance For An ICO

The incorporation of KYC in the ICO world is because of true incidents because many investors and ICOs have suffered and many crypto scams worth millions of dollars have already occurred. Due to lack of proper regulatory measures and policies, fraudsters from both the investment and the ICO side have taken advantage of this loophole and this has resulted in some serious scams and money laundering using the ICO system. Any investor found undertaking money laundering activities will put all the involved entities to the investigation, including the ICO issuer. This narrows all the way to Anti

Money Laundering (AML), which is one of the basic requirements of KYC.

How One Can Ensure KYC Compliance

One can essentially ensure KFC compliance in several ways. For example, if you are offering a service or a product that makes it necessary for the client to walk in and register so that they can be allowed to purchase the product, then you can have all the information verified face to face. It's the same case in the digital world, whereby, if you are providing online services or offering products like ICOs, then the best option is to get the information from a third-party identity verification service provider.

The KYC procedures are based on the collection and keen analysis of the identification documents of an individual as well as the data about the funds used for the purchase. The main purpose of this lengthy procedure is always to deter the activities of criminals who want to use legitimate market platforms for fraudulent activities like tax evasion, terrorist funding, and money laundering. The crypto world has already experienced these malpractices and this has raised the need for good KYC compliance, to make sure that all things are streamlined and both parties are safe.

KYC steps

- **Verification of the client's profile**

    Before beginning the KYC process, just ensure that you have a copy of your identification card and any valid document like a passport in electronic form, for the purposes of uploading. These personal details are legally required and both parties must provide this data in the ICO investment contracts.

- **KYC verification**

    Your personal ID is then compared with the data in your profile and any mismatch will be automatically detected by the automatic compliance check. At this stage, make sure that you provide the right information and let your profile and documented information be the same.

- **Video verification**

    At this stage, you should be ready with your ID for video identification, where you will be asked to display all your documents in the video call. Make sure that your ID document is still the same as what you used in step one. You can schedule a video call, but if the agent is available at that moment, then you can proceed with the video call immediately. The agent will then ask you several questions to verify your identity.

- **Digital signature**

  This is always the last step, and once the agent has fully verified your identification, you will then digitally sign. Mostly, a code is sent to you via mobile text within a few minutes. Feed the code into the system and the process will be completed.

Sometimes this process maybe daunting and tiresome, but the level of complexity will depend on the protocols that have been set in place by your token provider. However, this is a very important step because it ensures that, as a contributor to the ICO project, you are fully protected. With the KYC verification procedure, you are always sure that not only is your project secured, but also that you, as a token buyer, are protected from any possibility of anyone claiming that the resulting funds are not legitimate.

Crypto wallets

A crypto wallet is simply a digital wallet that is used to receive, send, or store digital currencies like Bitcoin or Ethereum, among other currencies. Most of the coins have an official wallet where they are stored or a third-party wallet that has been approved where one can store the digital coins.

Ideally, they are just like normal leather wallets in real life, used for carrying cash or our credit cards. The only difference is that the cryptocurrency wallets are in a virtual form. However, this virtual wallet, unlike the traditional wallet, tells you the balance that you have, your last expenditure, and such things that your leather wallet cannot tell you. Like digital applications, cryptocurrency wallets are smarter in the sense that they combine all the benefits of your physical wallet with more flexible and sophisticated features. With just one wallet, one can hold many digital currencies without ever worrying about something like running out of space.

As a cryptocurrency investor, you must familiarize yourself with how the wallets work so that once you acquire your tokens; you can have a smooth ride in trading in the ICO world.

The Working Mechanism Of Cryptocurrency Wallets

Cryptocurrency wallets work in the same way as a safety deposit box that you use to store your treasures like jewelry, certificates, or a will. You cannot afford to lose the key of such a box because it means that you will essentially lose ownership of the expensive possessions therein if the key falls into the wrong hands.

Cryptocurrency wallets work in this manner, only, instead of having physical keys, you will have a digital keycommonly known as a master key. Some people refer to these as private keys. They always come in the form of hexadecimal codes and they may look like this:

2940447a4ed5eef7f46bcc185cb2f21d2a8bffcde5418156a9d1a44aa137558

At first glance, they may seem to be complicated and daunting to understand, but with time, you will master them. When investing in ICO tokens or any other digital assets, make sure that you secure your wallet by taking care of your private key. You will always need the key to get access to your assets and authorize transfers from your wallet. So always keep your key in a safe place where you can easily retrieve it any time you need it.

Where Can You Get A Cryptocurrency Wallet?

You can easily get cryptocurrency wallets by signing up for one of the wallets. The cryptocurrency wallets are available in the following forms.

- **Desktop**

    These are wallets that are downloaded and stored on a laptop or PC and they are only accessed through the computer on which these wallets were downloaded. Desktop wallets are very secure, but this security can be compromised if your computer gets a virus or is hacked. But generally, desktop wallets are some of the safest wallets that you can use.

- **Online wallets**

    This kind of wallet runs in the cloud and one can access it using a computing device from any location. They are easy to access and more convenient, but the key is stored online by a third party and this makes it more prone to hacking.

- **Mobile**

    These wallets run on an application installed on your mobile phoneand they are very convenient because they can be used in any place to carry out ICO token-related transactions.

- **Hardware**

    These ones are different from software wallets because the private key is stored on hardware like a USB device. Although, with the hardware wallet transactions are still made online, there is better security with this kind of a wallet because everything is stored offline. The user just needs to plug in the hardware to an Internet-enabled device from any place and then he or she can make transactions.

Single Currency Or Multicurrency Use?

Bitcoin is the most known digital currency but many altcoins have emerged, each with a unique infrastructure and ecosystem. But the good news to those investing in several ICOs is that there are some wallets that support several coins. You do not need to have a separate wallet for your coins; you simply must set up a multi-currency wallet which will effectively enable you to concurrently use several coins from one wallet.

Are the crypto wallets secured?

Cryptocurrency wallets have been built to be very secure, although the exact level of security will differ from one wallet to another. But in general, like your usernames and passwords, the security of your wallet is ensured by strictly following best security practices. Just to guide you, these are some of the practices to secure your wallet:

1. **Obtain a secure wallet**

    With many cryptocurrency wallets available out there, it is wise to locate a wallet that is secured above what is offered by common wallet providers. Some wallets are now incorporating encryption techniques to add extra privacy to private keys.

2. **Use cold storage technique**

Users should have at least two wallets, but the number should depend on the amount of crypto funds that a user has. One wallet should be strictly for transactional and trading purposes while the other wallet should be used only for secure storage of the ICO tokens. This type of wallet, that is only used for storage and never involved in any transaction, is usually referred to as a cold storage wallet. Always ensure that in the trading wallet, you have only a few ICOs that are sufficient for your current trading activities.

3. Wi-Fi wisdom

Always be cautious about the sites you visit online using a device that has ICO wallets in it. Risky Wi-Fi, and some malicious websites, may put your wallet to risk. Also, remember that you should attend well to this device and never lend it to any person.

4. Gone phishing

In the crypto world, there are many phishing scams through emails or Google Ads. Phishing scams are very common, so always ensure that the emails you receive from the wallet companies always have their domains spelled out clearly and never look for their web addresses by clicking on a Google Ad.

5. Turn off any auto updates

You should turn off the auto updates for all your applications related to the crypto sphere because most of the application bags have the potential to cause harm to the wallet owner.

6. Double check all the addresses

It is always important to make sure that you have double checked all the addresses that you are sending any payments to. This is because there are malicious programs that can copy the procedures and then paste them to a different address belonging to the attacker.

Which are the best wallets?

The number of wallets is increasing every day and users have many options to choose from. However, before you settle your mind on which wallet to use in your ICO investment, just consider these following key things:

- Are you planning to invest in several ICOs or one?

- Do you need to access your digital wallet from any place or will you use it only when at home?

- Will you use your wallet for everyday purchases or are you interested in just buying and holding the coins as your investment?

Having asked yourself those few questions and having assessed your requirements keenly, then you can easily settle on which wallet will serve your interests well and by this, you will be able to choose the most suitable wallet.

Some of the best crypto wallets for ICO tokens:

1. **MyEtherWallet**

   This is one of the most popular wallets in the crypto world. It can be effectively used to buy, sell, and store the ERC20 tokens that have been obtained from ICO token sales. It is one of the most accepted wallets because is a wallet available online in addition to providing an offline wallet at the same time.

2. **Jaxx**

   This is another awesome wallet. It can hold, trade, and control your Bitcoin, Litecoin, Ethereum, Augur, and dozens of blockchain-based assets. It gives you complete control of your key, on top of having simple but great features.

3. **Trezor**

   This is a hardware wallet that offers a very secure way of keeping your coins safe from hackers and malware. Its most conspicuous features are cross-platform support and the OLED display.

4. **KeepKey**

   This is yet another hardware wallet that secures Ethereum, Bitcoin, Litecoin, and other tokens. It also offers a USB connection as one of its unique features.

5. **Exodus**

   This a multi-digital assets wallet and the first desktop wallet to have an inbuilt Shape Shift that allows for easy and fast conversion of various cryptocurrency tokens and altcoins. It also enables one to store the private key in an application that has a user interface which is customizable.

Legal Status Of ICOs In Various Countries

Currently, most ICO projects are defining themselves simply as presale program tokens. But from a legal point of view, they are most like selling early access to online games. Project owners tend to use the terms "mass sale" and "donations" instead of ICO so that they can escape from falling under the stock trading companies' category.

Determining the legal status of an ICO in your country is beneficial because, without a good legal framework, few investors from the real economy sector will be interested in investing their funds in ICO startups. Without a good legal framework, ICO tokens will be unattractive and this may limit the development potential of this sector.

On this issue, others still believe that the industry will be better without regulations because the authorities will not interfere with the ICO projects into which the investors are chipping in their funds. The downside of this issue is that with the absence of a good legal framework between token sellers and the investors, the ICO niche remains open for scammers who are always ready to profit from the investors who dream of making money from the tokens they purchase.

Perceived Challenges With ICOs

Many countries are reluctant about ICOs mainly because there are no good regulatory mechanisms put in place and technically, they represent a regulatory workaround. The issue behind this is that instead of seeking an initial public offering, businesses can be funded without any regulatory requirements, due diligence, time, or any fiduciary permission compared to the traditional IPO requirements. This peer-based system offers funding opportunities to ICO startups that would not be eligible for funding through the traditional approach.

Many countries argue that this approach is very comparable with fraud, and this is the main reason some countries like South Korea and China have banned the selling and creation of ICOs in their countries because there is a big door that scammers can use to defraud innocent investors in the ICO sector. Meanwhile, many countries are pursuing changes to their policies so that they can codify adherence to anti-money laundering issues. On top of this, if an ICO relates to flat currencies or property transfer, this may be essentially dealing with securities and this causes effects on the securities' integrity and taxation issues.

Progressive Countries In Terms Of ICOs

Applicability of ICO products, professional support teams, and extensive marketing campaigns on top of well-organized documentation are still insufficient for an ICO to succeed. Choice of jurisdiction is another vital aspect. The most favorable and progressive jurisdictions towards ICOs and the crypto sector are Singapore, the US, Scotland, Switzerland, and several more nations. Such countries that are supportive of the ICO have well-dictated procedures that give ICO projects a legal entity and tax legislation and this makes them friendly and favorable to the ICO startups.

Vitalik Buterin's Ethereum is an example of how Switzerland is favorable to crypto companies. The Swiss government has a good predisposition towards ICO startups because of their significant contribution to the economy of the country. Favorable conditions for the development of new crypto startups are the main reason why many cryptocurrency-based companies have been established in Switzerland. Even though Switzerland is one of the most ICO-friendly countries, most of the European Union members remain adamant and they are not the best choice for ICO-related ventures. One of the greatest challenges in these countries is the data protection laws whereby the financial companies must delete all information of transactions that have been processed by the clients from the database whenever a client requests it. But in the blockchain, one of the distinctive features is that information cannot be deleted and this is always interpreted as a violation of data protection laws.

Singapore is another good country but the charges may be high. The government is well-disposed to technology and it is very favorable to ICO investments, although Hong Kong is cheaper and a better choice than Singapore. However, they have very strict taxation policies. Being the mother of the technology, the United States is very friendly to ICO investments and has excellent jurisdictions for the ICO, but this is exclusively for its residents. Nonresidents may be subjected to serious expenses and, in my experience, severe scrutiny.

These are just a few examples of the countries that have fully incorporated ICOs into their economic sector. As an investor, carry out some research to know the jurisdictions on cryptocurrency that have been established in your country. Before investing, make sure that your country is ICO friendly and, as an investor, make sure that you comply with the laws that have been established to govern ICOs in your country.

The Future Of ICOs In Various Countries

Currently, the cryptocurrency market is worth billions of dollars and, based on this capitalization, different nations have realized the importance of being involved in the crypto arena. Even the skeptics now have less to question about the prospects and benefits of this technology. Based on the potential gains in this sector, many nations are coming up with regulations that will have an effect on the crypto world.

The current unregulated nature of the crypto market makes it more exposed to excessive regulations that may have a chilling effect on the ICO development. This is because many countries are seeking to close all the loopholes, and as the countries seek to become leaders in the ICO world, more regulations are expected. While the upcoming regulations are expected to minimize the expected investment risks, the investors still must take responsibility for their investments or their due diligence when investing in ICO tokens.

Registration With ICO

Tokens or ICOs are gaining exceptional experience from institutions and individual investors as well. ICOs are also referred to as next-generation crowdfunding or new IPOs. However, the blockchain-based ecosystem is still new and lacks some standards, thus, registering and making some token sales may be tricky to some people. Here is a quick guide to help you in registering and participating in the sale:

1. Registering through the ICO project site itself

All the legitimate projects that use an ICO to raise funds have a website where they have a clear explanation of what the project is all about, their objectives, funds needed, how long the funding campaign will be, and all other necessary details. On this website, you can register for the ICO as an investor. You will have to fill in your information and verify all the details.

2. Get Ether or Bitcoin

To purchase ICOs, you need Bitcoins or Ethereum cryptocurrencies. Once you have these coins in your wallet, you can then visit the project's website where you will be presented with all the information needed; you can see the amount that has already been raised by the project and which is required for you to participate; you must then accept the conditions and terms of service in order for you to continue. From this point, you can then buy project tokens. The minimum amount that you are required to invest depends on the ICO you are interested in, but the common amount is always in between $10 and $100. This amount is always stated in the project's white paper and it can also be found on the project's website.

3. Move the coins to the wallet that you control.

This has been said countless times, that never keep your cryptocurrency coins in the wallet that was initially provided by the exchange. This is because, in the exchange wallet, your funds may be jeopardized because you have no complete control of your wallet.

4. Buy the Initial Coin Offering Tokens.

After registering for an ICO and having your funds available, all you must do is send the amount of the cryptocurrency you are willing to invest to the address of the ICO campaign that you have opted to invest in. The basic goal of every ICO campaign is always to get money and for this reason, the process is not trivial and the project website provides clear guidelines to the investor.

5. Accuracy

When sending your funds, be careful and always ensure that you double check the website address because theremight be fraudulent ICO websites on top of your Google search outcomes. They resemble the actual website but several symbols in the address are different.

6. Get ICO tokens to your address

You will then receive the new tokens that you have purchased into your wallet's address and if it does not happen instantly, be patient for a while. The time it takes for you to receive the tokens depends on the campaign, and sometimes it may take even weeks before you receive the tokens. Also, to keep yourself updated, communicate with your fellow ICO investors in various forums and dedicated platforms. Sometimes, you may not be able to trade the tokens immediately after receiving them, but this depends on the rules established by the ICOs. The time to wait, when to begin trading, and any other necessary information is always provided on the website of the project.

What is gas in ICO?

Gas is the cost that is used to facilitate transactions in Ethereum, usually in the form of Szabos. (One Szabo is 1/1,000,000 of an Ether). The price of the gas for every transaction based on what is needed toturn the complete the process based on the EVM (Ethereum Virtual Machine Code) and the idea is always to limit the loops. For example, 0.00001 Ethers or 10 Szabos, also known as 1 gas can, execute a given line of command effectively. If the Ether balance in your account is insufficient to run the transaction or send the message, then the action is considered to be invalid; to avoid this, always ensure that you have a handsome Ether balance in your account when carrying out a transaction.

The amount of gas used depends on how heavy the command being executed is. For example, if you want to send 1 Ether to another person, the total cost of the transaction will be 1.00001 Ether. This is just an example of a simple code. If you run a heavy code, for example, forming a contract based on the future price of Ether with another person, more gas will be consumed because several complex codes must be executed.

MetaMask Wallet

The broad Ethereum community has recently come up with MetaMask, which is a new tool that is able to bring Ethereum to the user's browser via a plugin that is currently available for Google Chrome. This tool essentially enables one to run Ethereum dApps in the browser without the need to run a complete Ethereum node.

Benefits of MetaMask

Using MetaMask, the Ethereum system has been made very accessible to average consumers and this has been a very smart move. It is evident that the Ethereum ecosystem has many advancements to offer, but many people find it difficult to adapt to them because even accessing the dApps remains challenging to many because you have to run a complete Ethereum node. The MetaMask tool thus brings great relief to the average ICO investor because this tool has bridged this gap.

MetaMask addresses most of the problems experienced by common people because the plugin allows the user to access the dApps directly from the Google Chrome. This alone is agreat improvement since doing so has been a great challenge to many people because the dApps were not appealing because of the complicated process involved.

MetaMask also provides a secure identity vault to the user, thus allowing them to manage their identities across various websites, and these identities can also be used to sign the blockchain transactions. This tool also has a convenient user interface that presents things well, thus lowering the barrier to entry and usage as far as dApps and Ethereum are concerned. MetaMask is expected to bring the Ethereum ecosystem a notch higher in the coming months and years.

Chapter Five: Things to Avoid

Just like any other cryptocurrency, ICOs come with risk, and to make a sound investment into an ICO, you must perform due diligence. There have been many initial coin offerings that have failed for various reasons such as the token being offered not offering utility or security, and the company being unable to achieve a growth in price. ICOs are mostly underrated but have great importance as they represent huge returns on investments.

In ICOs, tokens are used as a medium of information exchange using a token-based model which implements blockchain technology. A company will experience greater demand through numerous buyers obtaining the altcoin. The more buyers and holders of a certain altcoin, the greater the demand and user base that company will experience. Therefore, crowdsourcing is done through token sales rather than direct interaction between buyers and users.

For instance, when 5,000 new users sign up and purchase tokens in an ICO, the financial "get" from the purchase of tokens is not only used as the first funding of a project but also to expand the value of the tokens in question. One example of this is the Bancor ICO, which took in over $153M in its ICO. These early buyers of the Bancor token are the most likely future users and adopters of the core protocol and services that Bancor provides, as well as the support team that will help sustain it.

Exit Scams

Despite the popularity of ICOs, coupled with successful projects, there have been several exit scams which seem to be rising daily. An exit scam is a fraudulent practice by unethical cryptocurrency promoters who vanish with investors' money during or after an ICO. Exit scams happen in a very simple way: first, promoters launch a cryptocurrency platform based on a promising concept. Then the ICO raises money from various investors for a specified period before disappearing, leaving investors in the lurch, unfortunately, this is a worrisome trend in the world of ICOs and cryptocurrencies and will end up tarnishing the reputation of ICOs for quite some time to come. It is difficult to trace scammers in these exit scams due to the decentralized, anonymous, and regulation-free operations of the virtual currency ecosystem. Some recent ICO exit fraud examples include Bitcoin, PlexCoin, and Confido. All these projects raised a small amount of money before effectively calling it quits and disappearing altogether. In 2018 alone, a total of $8.4m has been stolen to date, but the amount of stolen funds remains small compared to seemingly legitimate projects raising $50m or more.

Due to increased exit scams, ICOs have been discouraged and burned on various platforms. Investors have been warned by the U.S Securities and Exchange Commission (SEC) of the presence of scammers who utilize the ICOs to generate interest by driving up the value of the coins. ICO and cryptocurrency advertisements have been banned on various social media platforms including Facebook, Google, Snapchat, LinkedIn, and Twitter due to increased scams and the incredibility of their operations. Chinese Internet platforms Baidu, Tencent, and Weibo have also prohibited ICO advertisement. The Japanese platform Line and the Russian platform have similar prohibitions.

The SEC has also acknowledged that ICOs "may provide fair and lawful investment opportunities." The UK Financial Conduct Authority has also warned that ICOs are a very high risk and speculative investments, are scams in some cases, and often offer no protection for investors. The European Securities and Market Authority(ESMA) notes the high risk associated with ICOs and the risk that investors may lose all their currencies.

Identifying Exit Scams

Identifying exit scams in their early stages can save investors a lot of investments. Although it is evidently tough to recognize a dubious ICO, investors can monitor the ICO using the following key points before making an investment decision.

1. **Team Credibility**

   Accountability and ownership have been the biggest challenge in the ICO world, with every developing ICO looking promising at first for investors but later turning out to be an exit scam. Investors should, therefore, verify the credentials of the crypto team before investing their hard-earned cash. Investors should be aware that these fraudulent schemes are set up with huge starting capital. Therefore, they can do a lot to assure prospective investors of their credibility including buying likes, tweets, and followers on various social media platforms to build fake online credibility. They should perform a rudimentary check on ICO sponsors and on the promoters of cryptocurrency projects and the kind of networks they subscribe to.

2. **Extravagant Return Projections (too good to be true)**

When the deal is too sweet, think twice. An ICO promising an unimaginable return on an investment is definitely an exit scam. For instance, BitConnect promised a steady one percent daily return on an investment which would transform an initial investment of $1,000 into a return of more than $50 million within three years, attracting numerous investors despite the warning of a Ponzi scheme by Ethereum founder. Unfortunately for them, BitConnect abruptly shut down its lending and exchange services in January 2018 after experiencing a meteoric rise and burgeoning client base since its ICO in December 2016. The market cap of BitConnect, which exceeded $2.7 billion in December 2017, suddenly tanked to $17 million by March 2018, leaving investors with huge loses. Investors should think critically before making an investment decision.

3. Document Standard

Documentation is key in identifying fraudulent ICOs. The white paper is the key document explaining how an ICO project should function based on its design. Potential exit scams are usually characterized by unclear and ambiguous white papers. This should be a red flag to prospective investors.

4. Non-existent Working Model

Does the cryptocurrency project have a bare-bones working model? If it is a concept-only, non-existent product, then it probably will not function. ICO project promoters should prove that their developments function effectively and therefore can be worth investing in. Investors should clearly understand the functionality of a certain project before capitalizing on it.

5. Severely Promoted Offerings

A new ICO can be heavily promoted through expensive full-page ads, celebrities, and paid bloggers to relay false information. These are signs of exit scams and investors should be very careful when investing in such ICOs. Basically, it comes down to a renowned investmentadvice—if you do not understand the business of the company, and do not trust the people behind it, don't invest in its shares. The same holds true for cryptocurrency projects.

Multi-Level Marketing Systems

Multi-Level Marketing Systems are also fraudulent schemes in the world of ICO and should be completely avoided by investors. Multi-Level Marketing Systems work based on Multi-Level Tokens (MLT) which are inbuilt in the system. MLT is an ERC20 token built on the Ethereum blockchain. The token is a derivative structural product that gives token holders the right to acquire income out of the increased value of Ethereum. Token holders will also earn "coupon revenue" from a bonus program built into the token's smart algorithm. The bonus is earned through referrals; therefore, you are encouraged to convince friends and family to buy the tokens, in order for you to earn. Many Multi-Level Marketing Systems are fraudulent schemes where the bonus earned is not usually paid out, but rather, the investors disappear with the income received during referrals.

The Multi-Level Marketing System way of operation can be equated to a Ponzi scheme, which is a fraudulent investment promising high rates of return with little risk to investors. The Ponzi scheme generates returns for older investors by acquiring new investors. Just like the Ponzi scheme, Multi-Level Marketing Systems focus all their energy on attracting new clients to make investments through buying tokens. The income earned through the referrals is then utilized as a return on investment on the project's founders. A constant flow of new referrals is necessary for the scheme to sustain itself, together with the founders. When this flow runs out, the scheme falls apart, leaving token buyers with huge losses and in disarray.

Characteristics of Multi-Level Marketing Systems

It is simple to identify and avoid fraudulent Multi-Level Marketing Systems since they share the same characteristics listed below

- Guaranteed profits, coupled with few risks involved
- High returns, inconsiderate of prevailing market conditions.
- Investments that are not recognized by the Securities and Exchange Commission (SEC)
- Secretive investment strategies
- Clients having difficulties accessing their returns on investments in terms of money

Regulation

Following increased frauds associated with ICOs, including cyber thefts using Multi-Level Marketing Systems and trading halts due to exit scams and possible market manipulation, different countries have setup various regulations which are continually changing. Cryptocurrencies are based on distributed ledger technologies enabling people to acquire or transfer their cryptocurrencies directly to another person without the need of an intermediary. Therefore, they are exposed to fraud. It is difficult to regulate ICOs and cryptocurrencies using a central authority since they can easily be moved across national and jurisdictional boundaries. However, countries have developed varied approaches to regulate ICOs and cryptocurrencies, depending on the nature of the cryptocurrency.

Controlling cryptocurrencies can be broken down into two forms: utility tokens and asset-backed tokens. Utility tokens hold more value than asset-backed tokens since they are essential for the holder to exchange a token for a good or service in the future, for example, Bitcoin. Asset-backed tokens may have value because there is an underlying asset which the holder of the token can attribute a value to. In most countries, asset-backed tokens are regulated, rather than utility tokens, which are not prone to fraud. ICO regulation is still under development in most countries including Australia, Canada, and France. Countries that have already developed and implemented ICO regulations are the United States, United Arab Emirates, Switzerland, Gibraltar, and New Zealand. In China and South Korea, all ICOs have been banned completely. Owing to the difference in regulations per country, ICO investors must analyze which countries to sell their coins or tokens in based on set regulations, therefore increasing the complexity in trading cryptocurrencies. Prospective purchasers of cryptocurrencies also need to understand regulations in each country before engaging in any transactions.

The Gibraltar British Overseas Territory Financial Service Commission is in the processes of developing a framework to implement a worldwide regulation governing cryptocurrency transaction to eliminate the complexity of transactions due to different regulations in each country. Investing in cryptocurrencies and Initial Coin Offerings (ICOs) is highly risky and speculative. Investors should be careful not to get scammed by identifying exit scams early enough using the key points we have mentioned above. Additionally, Multi-Level Marketing Systems should totally be avoided as they are fraudulent ways to benefit initial investors. Whether the development and implementation of regulations will help curb scammers in the ICO world, time will tell.

Chapter Five: Wrapping It Up

If you had purchased $100 of BTC on Jan 1, 2011, it would have cost you $0.30 per BTC, amounting to 333.33BTC. Seven years on and BTC has hit an all-time high of $11k, exchanging at $9,315.28at the time of writing. Assuming you had kept your 333.33 BTC, they would be worth an incredible $3 million today. That is not a bad return for a $100 initial investment. Just like BTC, Initial Coin Offerings (ICOs) may have similar profits, butonly if carefully traded. In this chapter, we are going to discuss stages and tips in investing in ICOs.

Step in ICO Trading

1. **Research Extensively on Upcoming ICOs**

   Extensive research is vital in ICO trading since it is the only means by which an investor is guaranteed a return on his or her investment. An investor should look at resources or outlets that feature the latest ICOs. Knowing which ICOs are coming up will enable an investor to plan, especially for ICOs that have a whitelist. A whitelist ICO enables prospective investors to register in advance to participate in the ICOs, which are usually hallmarks of popular ICOs that have a limited number of coins to offer. The best websites to research upcoming ICOs are Top ICO List and ICO watchlist. At the time of writing, Top ICO List had placed TRIPBIT, COTI, and Qurrex as the top lucrative upcoming ICOs to invest in, while ICO watchlist had noted Payera, Xsolus,and Global Reit as the top upcoming ICOs. Therefore, prospective investors should carry out extensive research before deciding on which ICO to invest in.

2. **Act Diligently**

   In the previous chapter, we discussed how ICOs are prone to frauds such as exit scams and Multi-Level Marketing Systems. Due to this reason, investors should perform their own research to ascertain that an ICO is a good and credible project and hence avoid being defrauded of their hard-earned investments. Research done should involve reading reviews and analysis done by others to verify the potential of the ICO. There are so many good ICO review resources that can be accessed at Crush Crypto and Reddit websites.

3. **ICO Participation Process**

The ICO participation process entails three main steps.

a. Opening an Exchange Account

After extensive research and assurance in the credibility of an ICO, the next step is to open an exchange account to participate in the ICO process. The account should be able to accept fiat cryptocurrency to convert the domestic fiat currency into popular cryptocurrenciessuch as Bitcoin (BTC) or Ethereum(ETH).

b. Opening a Wallet Account

A wallet is essential to participate in an ICO. Participating in an ICO requires an investor to send BTC and ETH from their personal, private wallets. If they send it from an exchange, they will not be able to access the ICO tokens since the transfer originates from the wallet of exchange and, technically, they do not own any wallets in an exchange. Note, exchange accounts such as Poloniex, Bittrex, and Kraken are not personal wallets. There are numerous wallets available but the most recommended wallet is MyEtherWallet (MEW).

c. Follow the ICO Instructions to Trade

In most ICO trading platforms, a step-by-step guide to participating in the ICO is usually provided. A means of communication is also provided for the latest updates and to answer questions in real-time. Investors should ensure they follow the instructions to participate correctly.

4. Exchange to Trade ICO Coins

You should exchange coins to make substantial profits. You can hold coins for the medium- to long-term, depending on your price target i.e. (two times, three times,10x the capital. Alternatively, you could just flip the coin and sell it once it reaches an exchange that usually lists an ICO. Also, if you missed out, an ICO can be bought at an exchange.ICO coins can be listed on various platforms such as Ether Delta, Bittrex, Poloniex, and Binance.

Tips on Trading ICO Coins

After you've opened an account, let's now go over some of the essential tips in trading ICO coins for maximum profits.

- **Have a Reason for Entering each Trade**

    You should only start a trade when you know why you are starting and have a clear strategy afterward. Not all traders make gains from trading since the trade is a two-way traffic, i.e. for everyone who benefits, someone else loses on the other side. You should also understand the risk involved in trading and the risk of costly mistakes.

- **Focus on Coins that are on Reputable Sites**

    Coins from reputable sites guarantee you of their credibility. Trading in non-reputable coins is risky as they are associated with fraudulent schemes to extort traders of their hard-earned investments. As discussed above, sites such as Top ICO list and ICO Watchlist are renowned for dealing with credible coins.

- **Target and Stop when Starting a Trade**

    For each trade, you must set a clear target level for making a profit and more importantly, a stop-loss level for cutting losses where the trade will be closed. It is important to consider several factors when choosing a stop-loss level correctly. Most traders end up taking huge loses because they are unsure of the top level.

- **Do not put all Your Eggs in one Basket.**

    To be a profitable trader, you must manage your risk by looking at the peak of the movement. You should look for small profits which will eventually accumulate to large profits. You should spread your risk across your portfolio. For example, you should never invest more than a small percentage of your portfolio in a non-liquid market with very high risk. Also, invest with various cryptocurrencies such as Bitcoin and Altcoins which have inverse relationships, i.e. when the value of the Bitcoin rises then Altcoins lose their value against Bitcoin and vice versa. In this way, you are guaranteed a profit in the volatile market common with Bitcoins.

- **Secure Bonus Tokens**

    Most ICOs tend to offer some sort of bonus to incentivize investors to contribute early. For the LiveEdu pre-ICO, for instance, there was a minimum required investment of $3. However, investing $50 or more qualified you for a bonus of at least 25 percent. Savvy investors should look to get involved in ICOs from the pre-ICO stage. If you can get a bonus, then you will receive extra tokens for your initial investment.

- **Hold, Sell, Hold Some More**

    This is a very good idea to increase your investments. For instance, on receiving your tokens, it is wise to exchange them for other cryptocurrencies such as ETC or BTC. The cryptocurrency market is highly volatile and dynamic and you can release a higher return on investment.

- **Set Goals and Place Sell Orders**

    Always set your goals by placing sell orders. A successful strategy regarding this is placing very low buy orders. For instance, the Augor coin was down to 25 percent of its value. After a short while, the market recovered slightly and anyone who had low buy these low orders could easily double or triple their investment. Placing buy orders requires special care .Do not wake up when you are far away from the market to find your buy order is suddenly higher than the current market price!

- **Buy the Rumor, Sell the News**

    ICO trading requires you to always be informed on the current trends. When major news sites publish articles, it is usually at exactly the right time to actually get out of the trade and you will realize an immense return on investment.

- **Enjoy the Investment Process**

    Enjoy the dynamism of the whole investment process and this will enable you to put your ego aside, which is necessary for making profits. The goal here is not to be right on your trades, but to make a profit. Do not waste resources (time and money) to try to prove that you should have entered that trade. Remember, there is no trader who never loses at least sometimes. The equation is simple— get the total profits to be higher than the total losses.

- **Keep It Simple**

    While investing in ICOs, it is important to minimize over thinking and the worry of losing your hard-earned investments. Also, think critically about the most suitable ICO investment for you after extensive research.

Conclusion

I hope this book will clearly guide you as you make your next investment step in the ICO world. Always remember to be extremely careful when investing in ICOs as they can be fraudulent schemes. ICOs provide a means by which startups avoid the costs of regulatory compliance and intermediaries, such as venture capitalists, banks, and stock exchanges. Therefore, they can be a great means to start a company.

References

1. (https://masterthecrypto.com/guide-to-ico-investing/)
2. (https://bitcoinmagazine.com/guides/what-ico/)
3. (https://www.bloomberg.com/news/articles/2018-04-19/as-bitcoin-plunged-these-crypto-hedge-funds-kept-making-money)
4. (https://blockgeeks.com/guides/initial-coin-offering/)
5. (https://medium.com/@guy.phipps123/a-brief-history-of-icos-9e57f8550ad4)
6. (https://hackernoon.com/understanding-initial-coin-offerings-icos-a61064170150)
7. (https://medium.com/@icoformula/icos-and-the-importance-of-timing-68736a3728db)
8. (https://medium.com/zen-blog/how-to-understand-icos-2e3d09cf0c04)
9. (https://www.coinannouncer.com/beginners-guide-participating-ico-using-metamask-ether-wallet/)
10. (https://medium.com/the-mission/ico-101-how-to-participate-in-an-ico-made-with-ethereum-cf57516183f6)
11. (https://cryptocurrencyfacts.com/how-to-create-a-custom-token-in-myetherwallet-how-to-add-a-token/)
12. (https://cointelegraph.com/bitcoin-for-beginners/how-to-buy-ico-tokens-beginners-guide#7-once-you-have-your-ico-tokens-figure-out-how-to-store-them)
13. (https://medium.com/@Hash_Rush/a-newbies-guide-to-ico-participation-purchasing-your-first-cryptocurrency-287916c1179)
14. (https://cryptopotato.com/9-must-tips-securing-crypto-wallet/)
15. (https://medium.com/@Crowdwiz.io/how-does-a-cryptocurrency-wallet-work-and-how-to-create-one-f234c6ec076f)
16. (https://cryptocurrencyfacts.com/what-is-a-cryptocurrency-wallet/)
17. (https://cryptocurrencyfacts.com/tip-consider-buying-the-token-after-the-ico/)

18. (https://blog.datum.org/why-datum-requires-identity-verification-for-our-token-sale-159dcfb139d0)

19. (https://shuftipro.com/blogs/icos-and-know-your-customer-kyc-compliance/)

20. (https://tokenguru.net/articles/how-to-start-trading-ico-tokens-and-get-maximum-profit/)

21. (https://www.google.com/search?q=how+to+know+whether+a+ICO+project+is+transparent&ie=utf-8&oe=utf-8&aq=t&rls=org.mozilla:en-US:official&client=firefox-beta&channel=fflb)

22. (https://medium.com/@sherbin/the-5-most-prospective-icos-for-investing-in-2018-105d21d4c2a5)

23. (https://cryptopotato.com/10-keys-evaluating-initial-coin-offering-ico-investments/)

24. https://steemit.com/cryptocurrency/@vincze95/how-to-maximize-your-cryptocurrency-profits-1

25. https://cryptopotato.com/8-must-read-tips-trading-bitcoin-altcoins

26. http://www.livebitcoinnews.com/number-of-ico-exit-scams-rises-but-amount-of-stolen-money-remains-low/

27. https://icowatchlist.com/upcoming

28. https://www.forbes.com/sites/laurashin/2017/07/18/how-to-speculate-in-icos-and-buy-tokens-an-easy-step-by-step-guide/#c4fb40c743aa

29. https://topicolist.com/

30. https://deadcoins.com/

www.ingramcontent.com/pod-product-compliance
Lightning Source LLC
Chambersburg PA
CBHW030038230526
45472CB00002B/570